Daydream Daughter

DAYDREAM DAUGHTER

Catherine Firestone

McClelland and Stewart

McClelland and Stewart Limited
The Canadian Publishers
25 Hollinger Road,
Toronto
Cover: Michael van Elsen
Printed and bound in Canada

For my parents

CONTENTS

DAYDREAM DAUGHTER

Daydream daughter
opens unseen horizons
for those who are willing
to be weaned on the unknown,

for those who wish to free
themselves from the padlock
fastened to the known;
Daydream daughter

will make minds for the dead
and undreaming out of her haze
and craze and daze, admitting light
as a dream-hole out of day;

so shall the real only be
the untimed, mimed mood
to release from restriction
the self-willed fantasy.

VALPARAISO

Somewhere farther, where time is a vanishing-
    point, lies the valley of Valparaiso
    where girls and boys become sovereigns
    and there are no slaves

Somewhere farther, where grief lapses joy
    wipes dark spots off sunflowers,
    the thieves are given before they steal,
    the ill-natured are courteous like queens

Somewhere farther, where earth neither
    dusts nor iron rusts,
    the spring-lock of love spades
    a staying soil

Somewhere farther, where gates open
    to Main-Street ideals
    and last year is always
    are we spanless and farthest

THE FLOWER-PANED ARCH

As I touch my neck
with ink-stained hands
the flower-paned arch
rings out the tongue and groove
       the words's wisp
acting as regent
the appointed rut, undeviating.
Will the world accept my contribution?
Lest dowdier throats take over
I will connect again, be drawn into
the era of effort.
       If you stamp your lips
on every relic, your belongings
will abide as headlines
binding you hand and foot
in a relay race
in which both history and hearsay
do part of the distance;
       as the whelp
of whalebone, they startle
thwack and climb the wall of time
like a creeper up a timbered block
kept at the height
       of its prime.

CONTINUUM

this is a finely-filled cemetery,
row re-echoes row and bone

bone, nothing bends the rock
that carries roots so far beneath

and yet lovers carry on the livelihood
left behind by croaked crones

and crooked, barren gents;
body to grit the lovers stock

the space between the worn stone
almost forgetting their abode

until the cider apple falls
when they would cross with coin

a fortune teller's hand
to gain a clue of life below;

this is a finely-filled cemetery
where graves are rocked cradles,

where the living keep up the sand-
blind's spirit in continuum of kind

SOLO

Solo sits; the organ has a defective
Valve, no hearers are near
      One player solitaire switches chairs
      He accelerates the handling
Of the queen's card,
Dissolved caoutchouc
      The unaccompanied pasteboard,
      He seems annoyed.
His upper eyelids droop
Like rubbish shooting down the chute
      The birdwide toucher flicks his wrist
      Inside the cinerary urn; without her
He puckers into wrinkles
Folds and bulges, he could go
      On the sick-list
      But he's too strapping
Like the pudding of pig
He's still stuffed with oatmeal and blood.
      As the hollowed-tree remnant of
      Coupling, he's a half-pier to most,
Fussing like the churlish blind
With a broken churn-staff.
      His elbow is a load on the table;
      She could reinsert herself
Maybe, but fear, the early curfew
Would intercept; dried fruit
      Of a seedless quality sits next
      The slender shade
Of the curly wading bird
Laid to rest

A VOICE ON PAPER

Is the steep face of rock hers?
Or is she fitted with faceless sights
which have fruited early

and claimed their sores?
While she has spelled out height,
direction, speed, and range

with a predictor's sure fire,
she loses touch with the whole of earth,
shuns a walk through the meadow stalks;

the girl who scrubs the tub
while eating her vanilla ice cream;
the infirm who set forth dimly,

daily; the wind which rasps and raps
like the sea's irritated bladder;
a kind trill of a word for mother.

What is this mess and muddle she is in?
Are these false steps which she
is making? As a time-server, as a time-saver

till all she feels is hollow delinquency?
Look to the jabbering earth o burning
vertigo: she's just a voice on paper

CLIMB THE MIND

Augustus Caesar says: let wine
loose your deep pool of tongue,
let the inborn fragments
of drooping ears be sung,
as a howling monkey's jaw
releases hood-shaped flowers
with the dung

Augustus Caesar says: a poet
is as good as his better half,
when he tells with
his clavichord of craft
that an utterly dry well
will spill again, give life
as water to a raft

The mood is meditation
climb the mind,
plant your existence
in the freed eye's giant line,
perhaps there is a vacancy
in a remoter grave
than time

YEVTUSHENKO

From hand to lip – fury, fury –
vodka and celery is what I served
you, mind to mind and man to woman
as we let the words move in
and every other inrush which stirred

Absorbed into the supreme spirit
of a second life, you have an actor's
allure, nursing fury with your tongues
like forceps, nippers and pincers
the business of seals, of shopkeepers

And of civil causes. To the night-hags,
your voice is like the night-cellar
and we, tucked into the underground
drinkshop get drunk on your poems
like child sucks

Such are the pinnacles for, the tunnels to,
the channels between us
and it is our parallel arrival
at the Root of Fury which allows us
to knot the node of a kiss

To condense the birth of a code

AS THE LAMP IS AGAINST NIGHT

the poem is against absence
as the lamp is against night
the poem is the man i don't know
the poem is the first and last
door, a crevice stuffed with
and pocketed by memory; the poem
pokes the dreams i've eaten
escorts the escarpments of space
containing nothing
but the brain's inquisition
and the new year. the poem
all day every day the poem
extends and under over music
the most intimate insurgent
white, a silhouette on the other
side, the poem provides is
brought to me as are brought
to me the blood-stones
from the hippopotamus-people.
the poem as fever's dividend
as the esparto grass in me
or when he's not here i write

AN IMAGINATION'S DISTANCE FROM THE ORCHARD

Because my own full sight bears down
on me
I am gathered an imagination's distance from
the orchard
From love made flesh; it is as if my mind kicks
in its own skin
With the weight and pain of growth
and so
Less giving, loves badly and would seem to
divide us;
I extend my reach only to find myself farther
from you.
This is not everyday life, the crumb and tuft
of everyone,
Luckily. I would have thought you'd make
a hasty retreat
As I am so slightly put together, as I make
short flights
Away from you so often, to shrink inside
my shroud
But you who are wise allow me to
strike loose
And you never shut the door upon me
when I return.
In this way, we have become one in the same
my skin
Is yours, your skin is mine even if only we
know it.
Do you remember the last time we conquered
the wet grass
When you split my toes to draw through them the axis
of eight blades?

Love is a large job especially with the first
coming of
New blooms and it is rarely that we let
the grass
Grow under our feet. Even still, when my own
full sight
Is not rubbing with harsh scraping noises against
itself,
We turn to each other, giving heed to our dignity
and stride
Of head, till next a sunstroke spots the leaves' lips
on tips of pasture land

THE HAUNTING-KEEPER

When I kissed the dead man bringing
bravery, enough to make an imperturbable
father proud, it was my death, too

yet I could not howl; we talked,
his voice rose grudgingly
from the stone which closed him under.

"Companion, it is as if all of me
has been smashed but death has committed
an error by leaving us imagination."

To which I replied: "As to logs
in the unsettled ocean, we hold onto panic
in front of death, yet my love for dreams

puts me out of danger as you prove
that dreams may pause for breath
(a decoy) but do not end."

"Dear attendant," he called,
"I see you as the graft from which I still
get sap, see you as god the healer

carrying my life on; we both have
somewhere to go.
Homeward now, I've said my peace,

the doorway's clear." "Friend," I
cried, "what may I call you?"
(He was more flesh than granite

to be sure.) "Child, do not limit
yourself to names or if you must, then
call me Dog or Fugue or the

Haunting-Keeper. Will you mop my brow
now, cover me up? Will you smile one more
ridge of a smile? Daughter, you defend me."

It was then that near-by footsteps,
had me scrambling
uncontrollably off as I grabbed

the soil of Haunting-Keeper's shadow
so that with it I could pack
a permanent pit in which to dream or live.

MOSAIC-MUSIC

O I have been radically intense
As Alice in the nightmare looking-glass
Solitary as a lunatic spirit
Without sanctuary
The caricature of declining hope
And yet I should like to be
Your summer's day pledge
Your peasant girl pleasure
Your eyes to illuminate the mind
And I should like to sail with you
To hear the mosaic-music
Of the youth which is truth
In Alexandria

FINGERING A MEANING

tricks grown skimpy; top hats empty
the play's not written but the act's begun

we've done with the dull and with the distracted
stare which locks people out, the likes

of us care to dare: we want to meet
we cross the room; the age of game has gone

our eyes' answerings run their course,
I dreamed of walking and I walked to you

we do not hide behind
a can or fan or gown or group

what in an hour will lie, a deluded heap;
we leap, to seek the same place –

all the while fingering a meaning, stunning
the meek and spiny-finned, what is left in

those around us: the damp, the deaf, the separate

I NACHITRIA YOU HIAMASKA

To the coach house
    Like coalmice we fly
I Nachitria you Hiamaska
    To the hutch of an outhouse where we've
Always been confined,
    For we are not like the others, day in
Day out as steady
    As a cobbler mending shoes; I Nachitria
You Hiamaska are
    Side-splitters, split to the side
Sometimes nut and dry
    Husk, and sometimes rose and juice-berry
I Nachitria
    You Hiamaska, do turn our skin, rind
And layer of bulb
    Around so that I, woman, rattle
At knifing
    You, man, fizz at knitting that shaggy
Woolen stuff
    (Do you sit here only to remember the arms
Of your mother?)
    What will our hybrid bring? No one
Will venture
    To grabble for a guess, no one says
What they really think
    Though I Nachitria you Hiamaska
Think we do
    So we say that we are each someone
Else's self
    Though in the interval of being us, we love

TO LET LOOSE THROUGH A LOOP-HOLE

To let loose through a loop-hole
Which we've cut out of the glass papered
Wall, slack, relaxed not tense or taut;
For so long, I hung only partly free
Tapped and knobbed with injury

Let go, let go, I will let go
With spittle at the lips, I yelp
The nays fall off, the yeas fall in;
Freedom is the object of the slit.
You renew the water in the bowl glossed

Like a glass-blown box through which
We've had to bite, through which
Our spliced strands and fleshings seep.
Now we can move about more readily, we've
Drudged but then doors do not fly open by

Themselves; openly, like an unclogged pit
Of drain, do we take up space,
Do we span from end to end
The spanless coves and bellied roads
And counterpoints; to let lingeringly loose

WALK THE PLANK

one can never say one has known it
love yet ever alters
as fast as I can copy down;
in an hour this minute is legend

already. in a day a child is bedded
with the jinx of germ or from Capitol
and university the work runs short of time
or draftsman draws off wrong lines,
or placards rise and cups fall;

these are managed
laboured healed repaired

but that you let feelings walk the plank,
helm down, that you doubt to body me, clear
signs of undecided, do have my pulse
return to zero. can the cloth have soaked
its full due to be wrung out so soon?

these are not managed
laboured healed repaired

for love is not as sure as birth,
a stronghold this noon is sandstorm this moon
for each is change, diverse as types
like life found at various depths of sea

PAPER DREAMS

Limp is the dream which goes unheeded
Leavened is the dream which goes as seeded, real

So it is not enough to paste together paper dreams
Because they may be torn too soon or creased

In costly crumple, filed away
Like catchwords in the heads of sleepers

And may on the balance sheet convey paper profits
Hypothetical, for show, entries owing;

So germ the tender plant, raise
A loving look from seed, be the doer

For we were not made to live with our souls
In straight-jackets, were not made to turn

Our backs on the sunset, on the road back
From the country, we were made to make, for

Limp is the dream which goes unheeded
Leavened is the dream which goes as seeded, real

HEATHCLIFFE (REFORMED)

1

Every passion is delivered as an angry bucket
from which
Every trodden body takes a gulp therefore you
fasten fear
Under every brow or skirt though not in mine I
am done
Up in you I am looked at from between your
eyes I am
You; from inside your power I gain mine we
hang from
Each other's hearts hang from each other's bellies
wild wild o
Such beautiful animals we recognize ourselves
as an entire
Armful of one and with chalk I proclaim it that
we (agitation's
Every moment no simple fairy tale) are the howl of
love wild wild
Lifelong inserting every burst whatever happens
shall proceed
Always even to defy the gravedigger as we set out in
this man
Of an afternoon to pin ourselves upon the heath—
birthright
Among the grasses or as they we too have a
mouthful
Of flowers: such is how the world collects us

2

But who are you now how you've changed hardly
can I
Believe it: you a gentleman with such soft
bringing
Entreating tender tender but there still as if it
hides the fierce
Coughing in the eyes I know it is but a change
of costume
Still you hunt me every time with your lurking
breath-fête
With your frenzied devil's suffering even when
you're not
Here; Heathcliffe (reformed) but the touch is
exactly the same
You unbutton my blouse as before we run off bellow
tremble hallucinate
Crucify just as before; minds wrapped together identical
disturbed continually
Swollen with a laughing called love wild wild
a vintage
For we the buzzing demons scream sometimes
mutely every
Welcome live sidelong in mid-air battle to
combine our
Souls' crusts thrust forward our whiskers tentacles
horns to be (to
This day) the increased revealing of love's most ample knife

THE ABSOLUTE CUBE OF SLEEP

She goes into the absolute
cube of sleep

like the potter stretching
the decisive boundary

on her revolving disc of dream
to make a baby-faced man

out of earth-pewter;
she doesn't have to tell

him anything:
his spirit is.

She goes into the absolute
cube of sleep

where eyes open
are as eyes shut

for fear of seeing too much,
seeing that man

as she would have him be
is never as he is.

With night washed of fervour
like gypsies' blood

she goes into the absolute
cube of sleep

to claim the unfinished face
like a letter with postscript;

nothing is impossible
and everything is real

she writes him into life.
May love begin where language ends;

we know if there were love
she would be mute.

I-KNEW-YOU-ONCE-BEFORE

From shantytown to the pearl islet
of Martinique: that's where we first met
where the mind-stuff fed on the milk
of almonds and on a fitting nudge
and nibbling of my grasses

into which he pushed off cautiously.
To make sure that this wouldn't end
quite that soon, he sent me a red balloon
and I sent him a gold globe
for he was the earth I lived on

"How unprepared I am will be without you"

I thought, all together
with this I-knew-you-once-before
certainty locked up in me as I stood
like a cock weather-wise by the woodpile,
having made quick doings of conquest.

And the question was: should we grub up
the stub by the root and clear some land
for us or go off, each on his own,
only to return home to the snug, steely
ganglion cells, bareheaded and ill-smelling

Only those who dare to make a change, live

He was a man of his word
and a notch in the bark confirmed it;
lumbering soon began on pearl islet
where a falling tree brought down
our neigh of peace

UNTIL THE DANDELION'S SEED-HEAD IS DEAD

Until
    the dandelion's
    seed-head is dead
Until
    we are taken in by this
    whole hoax of bone
Until
    we are stricken with
    the slipping loop of years
We shall clench this life
    with mits and fists
    and boxing gloves
We shall turn each day
    into a month to make the most
    of time's toke, each stroke
Until
    spring walks out
    on us like a tired lover
    who never bothers to look back

SEAGRAVES

looking at you
     a vision goes up my heart
looking forward
     to everything in store for us
I am not looking
     beyond you
as I'm looking into
     the seashine
     though fear the seagraves
when looking back
     is all that's left

L.A. PAVEMENT
For Robert Evans

begetter of images, etcher of life
through a lens, let me peel you
suitably out of the L.A. pavement,
let me press you out long enough to say
that you have stretched the joints
of my dreams like memory stretching to the time
to come; etcher of heart-throb, of death
splitting girls from men like rip-saw,
of love out of earth, of Tinsel
Town with rosebud rehearsed, all
that makes a thing what it is
from simple sketch to final frame
as in this rush of poem, a bird-call
for you are more than thing invented,
a hush in sleep, a howl in day;
I shall make you entire, I will not
give up what I have for what you have
(you would not wish that) but
I shall give you a sense of self, jointly,
wipe your brow at a swollen
moment, write our names in the spreading
sand as if on copperplate, until
I shall walk bang into you and we shall
know each other, retroactively

IN SINGLE FILE
For Jacques

Speak now, love in a coupled bustle, pluck
and follow through for after, the frost will bite
with lies and time will grow as thin as hair

with feathery spikes and shiny, floating patches; as
into life we are all droppers-in, it hardly
has the chance to grow than it has the chance to go –

Life is the lark it should be, so go off
to the courts and find your lady in limelight,
in a land of trimmings and superstar, go off

exhibit your wares, trade a well matched moment
as acutely as a horse-dealer, let the thick-soled
boot lend height to the actor in you

or be as simple as the single blond braid
delivering the daily paper; go off alone,
if you so please, in single file as all in the end

must – extend, splash, and dream of bodies open
or draw yourself in; go off, go on, go up
so that your last bone will not go out

with the annoyance of regret, for after
the frost will bite with lies
and time will grow as thin as hair

which heaves without a head.

FRATERNAL TWINS

Scarcely can we recall our old bones,
the way we used to be, alone
and as weak as a fish with no fin-spines,
alone, until we were hit by the stray bullet

      of each other's eyes. The days of watching
      walls or nothing at all have come to an end.
      You are the man who sets the slender
      blade of pipe to pitch life out of tale and

we are growing private by degrees. As long
as the dream holds out, we do,
for a dream cut off at the stem
leaves a depressed scar and a blunt end.

      But the lung of our dream cannot be blown
      out of wind; see how we can move the unmoving
      with our frank-pledge. Twin, the more you tie
      me to your cord, the more you set me free, instead

LET SAINTHOOD RING FOR GOLDILOCKS

Naked vocative, naked fox

Naked vocative
which moves through us,
which is the reservoir of oil in lamp
or ink in pen or good egg in
brain-fevered uterus

Naked fox
which makes inroads in us,
which is the perfect pucker
or streetwalker's wink or
loose strap under red slip

Sometimes we're one, sometimes
we're none, latently we're both of
them; there's no greater compliment
for a fifty-year-old than to be taken for
a hussy or for a twenty-five-year-old

To be the thought-potter, two-voiced vantage.
Let beauty stitch our twigs
together, let sainthood ring for Goldilocks,
the naked vocative,
the naked fox

IF AS YOU PULL OFF MY PURPLED STOCKINGS

if as you pull off my purpled stockings, you
pull me inshore with your ten oars, overtly
if you pump me up by the roots to you, then
am I loosened by your pulley's shaft

from the soft formless mass, we are pulse,
hugely, each successive drum up of mine
runs in the hum of your sinus, we pluck
as to a plant; we suck as to a pipe

and in this, you catch sight of a purveying
woman for I too pull my weight
as we put a spoke into the wheel
as we too pull into putted fire

but if you pull my leg and push
me away, I am pulled to pieces
to know that I have been a pullet
tugged till the first moult

only; for in such a push-button war
we both lose, feel the pinch
over us, as we have been soundless and deeper
than a falling lift;

and that, snappishly, to be purled upside
down and to get the push with the thrust
of horn, must direct me to pull back tightly
from the shooter and push out new roots

IN THE LIGHTHOUSE

She lives in the lighthouse   she sits
and she writes, undefeated or so
she likes to think   keeps winding
up her head for those even more
hours   keeps puffing up
the let's sing not fall asleep

Up to you, she bolts over your
body, so as to say one new thing
and (little by little) it is your
unearthed earth, a measure
of her sliding sand, the poem
somehow like a step-child
she can just abide
like a lover who won't leave her

and wrecked wanton or
wondrous it (against the undertow)
guards them both   perhaps once it
will guard you

MORE ROSE THAN RAT

Ideally, we would be more rose than rat
in similar key and free (eligibility

is the best matchmaker) and not
problem-children singing "Alleluia,

my world will be sold to the highest
bidder" or "if you don't give me

what I want, I'll leave." For ideally,
we would be more rose than rat

rallying for a hug and pun, re-inforcing
what a lover does with what a lover says

for we will have become part of bud
without the burden of rodent, its gnawing

glut, even if I am the painted lady, sometimes
sparse and perhaps I don't have everything

but you protest: "If you scratch the surface
you'll find it's only oil

but it doesn't mean to say
it's not good art."

MASTERLY ONE
For Nancy Cole

we are
Countries like a troupe of globe-trotters
running at a moderate pace
shingle to shingle we form a roof
if one stirs a single bone
the others crack at the jolted joint

we are
Committees moving in distinct stretches
like span-worms
as roundabout as a round robin
and yet we consign to ducks our muck
for treatment or safe keeping

we are
Couples set on a toll-gated jolly-boat
wishing to be accepted, acclaimed
with tussles one day
and tutti-frutti the next, downcast
uphill; to that co-equal sequel

but masterly
One
like a surprise packet
One
the tough rinded house-head
of its own skin
One
One-legged, one step, one kernel
can make the hard-shelled
fruit-stoned world turn

MISS RIGHT AND MASTER WRONG
For Tony

"Can you go, Miss Right?"
"To the show tonight, Master Wrong? If
        you toe the line, I might."
"Don't be so coy, Miss Right."
"You're just a boy, Master Wrong. And
        for how long, Master Wrong?"
"To see *King Kong*, Miss Right, it'll
        take all night, Miss Right."
"But it can't, Master Wrong, it'll
        give Dad such a fright."
"All right, then, till midnight,
        Miss Right."
"Okay, Master Wrong, let's hop along."
"Not hop along, Miss Right, spin in
        like a kite, to a drive-in,
        Miss Right."
"Oh no, Master Wrong, not here, I beg
        with a tear."
"But we're near, Miss Right, deary do,
        Miss Right."
"Do what, Master Wrong? But – Master Wrong,
        all I want is popcorn."
"Stay with me till morn, Miss Right."
"Now my dress is torn, Master Wrong."
"Don't look so forlorn, Miss Right."
"What will Dad say, Master Wrong?"
"That you've learned to play, Miss Right."
"Wrong, Master Wrong, that I've frizzled
        in a fray."

MINE IS AN INFREQUENT BELLY

Mine is an infrequent belly
Lasting out as support staff –

They, do I touch who love enough of me,
Sometimes; in our cubicle kept separate

He undoes my cover-alls, throwing me
Over his hip, the cross-buttock

Leads out, he is as high-flown as a
Pent-up limey long overdue

But he is well-made
And will not hasten as I

Let him trace a narrow mark
On my surface, we make slow

And regular progress, bending en route
Fuzz-ridden is the fusible wire;

They say that shrubs grow
Even on European waste lands.

THE PHILOSOPHER'S EGG

creation: broad-leafed blackbird
it's all because of the philosopher's
egg; such is the power

(the fresco depending
on the rhythm of the forehead in the
fingers and its hunger disturbed)

of the herbs: lifting the eye
joining the eye private eyes
that we all may feel

(out of the considerable
wiping of brows and despair's
hooting)

that there is more
to man than beard and clothing
more to me

(in the thousands of years
of alchemy from base arms
to gold wings)

and you
        (inside me)

LIKE TRAMPLED CHILDREN

It is always for your being
here beside me

too chilling your
not being here to have even the
simplest of conversations

you don't belong away from me –
then silence officiates; the rumour
is that memory is the slenderest
of consolations   wake up afraid
that each day I won't see you
if they won't let me; oh this rebellion
in the bones   I walk
into a b u r s t i n g tree
can I invite you to accompany
me: we can hide in our mouths
(no one will know) plant defiant roots
like trampled children and
as we always do
crumple our bodies into one
budding power
of carbon alcohol and
like gunpowder
we can go off with the loudest noise

it *is* always for your being
here beside me

TO FLUTTER THE DOVECOTS

As he did not like dowdy women
in fallen posture, but the hem
at the height of the helm and eyes
in a pool and thicket of blue chalk
to flutter the dovecots and a head
like yellow-tails in the hayfields,
hooped in holly, I called in the gardener
to tend to HIS cress and crest first:
after all, it was an open-air game
and we didn't wish
to infringe on the code of fair play,
after all, young ones can be shrews
on any stage; sometimes we'd meet and pass
like York and Lancaster, rivals
with reason, sometimes he'd exhibit
his cowboy skills with as much din and
hee-haw
as in the round-up of women
with a loose rein, sometimes I'd fill
the saddle bags evenly
with what we both felt, then
on a slate-coloured night
we'd strew the floor with rushes
at the annual northern festival
waiting for the guinea fowls to mate

SHADOWED BODIES

But if I call on you to be gentle with me,
do not refuse, greying cowboy, be it a
collective celebration and let us go on and
postulate through folksongs; let us be
shaken by each other, no matter how much or
how far, let us kick up these stored-up forces
that have gathered in the young barracks of
our shadowed bodies; let us, because we are
dead tired of touching empty eyes, go forward
toward that existence where men
name great silences or simply jump into bed;
let us adhere to our surf's passing, to its
created telling, let us bite each other's
fingertips, and hearing that behind the pil-
low, there might be a world, do not listen
too intently, if I call on you to be gentle
with me.

COWBOY AND PARTNER

before sundown, a cowboy cries I need
your shielding and I'm not about to give
you any of those sissy pardons, partner
      pussywillows or a portrait of,
      you are of such movement,
      ever ever softer though
      your backbone as reed's rod
      is strong; young sunup,
      I can lean on you
      without the fear of seeing
      sag like a sock
      your firm-stemmed shingle of stalk;
for even the broad-shouldered
snap the shield and crack the shell,
the strongest show weakness to themselves

TWO TRIBES

Two tribes
Floss-silk fingers or
Iron-yielding ones, she's ready as anyone
if life's as tangled as gypsies' hair
if life's as plump as apple pie
Floss-silk fingers or
Iron-yielding ones, she can wrench a sword,
rake the yard, empty the bin
like the man in the commercial
Floss-silk fingers or
Iron-yielding ones, she can flower
the leg of stocking to be spontaneous
not dutiful, she will not let
a chance slip to softly be
Two tribes
Little Bo-peep is a Bo-swell,
A Witwoman equal to Whitman
in this life
as knotty as warbattling bred
when needs are turned to warted weeds
as simple as a father asking diligently
if his son has made his bed

IDENTIFYING ITCH

i am so much you
i am no longer myself,
you are so much me
you are no longer yourself
identifying itch, birth-marked
we sense the stump of roof
and pile of sky like rootery
butted down on our necks
home to roost
we cannot move,
our lack of standing-ground
has us complain
until one of us clears a space
in the bathroom; greater
or more fundamental, we still
want to be with each other
and be ourselves,
so we learn to make
room to recoil
and room to mate

IN THE FABLE

I liked him – he talked in
terms of absolutes like I
would we were a little less heroic
though, our story hasn't reached
the stained-glass window after all

When my hours minus absence are you
when your hours plus presence are me
we show the beauty around ourselves
that which cannot be burned
down

And we know for certain that the Lighthouse exists that the Moonlight
exists Sun's Vigil on horseback
and God in us too
           affectionately yours,

AMORPHOUS

when not even thinking about him
helps or when it is almost impossible
to surrender oneself figuratively or when
even the lifting sun tows one under
or when one discards finger-nails and
toes as if it were a blessing or when
even the gigantic silence (beyond logic)
contracts space or when one would even
consider assassinating the most
guileless of squirrels and when then
it is best to push the eyelids shut
and staple the hands
to the almighty red-hot heart (just
in case) for it is
best then to be amorphous

OF WOUNDS

        The sun's never here
        when I need it most

Time for an asphyxiating scream
Let me love

        this hard day
        hard to want to be oneself

Before my eyes(and is it possible?)
words as visitors which dispirit

        I pretend to disappear
        but he's still there

If we are to succeed love me
(to repair my chipped wings) heavily

        We are almost
        extremities of one beginning body

which are intended to link syllables
as to (of wounds) step over and surpass
        them

IN CALLING HOURS

it certainly
isn't easy
to warehouse
old feelings,
like furniture

farewell to years
you waned,
but she
didn't want
any more

the hot bed's
a cold shower;
the walls
keep house
by themselves

lead down
to be
pulled up
who will
show up?

in calling hours
those who call off
      are echo
those who call on
      are sound

WE HAVEN'T GOT TIME TO MAKE SPACE

I've left you or you've left me
    or we've left one another
        whatever
we've broken the uniform hourglass
    in half, its grains break
        over the table
with a raw blow of stone-mass
    we've made a change for the
        worse
we haven't got time
    to make space with
        each other
though I still move at night
    towards would-be you. This is
        make believe
which has just stepped ashore, only it
    survives and anxiety dragging me
        (echo: xiety)
If I could create a new parish
    of a world how would I
        mould it?
If I could create a new fugue
    of a man how would I
        fashion him?
Futile to say. Once upon an evening
    you made a god of my
        light-fabric dress
once upon a morning, we complete
    our day alone. It's time to
        draw a hood
over my farm of a face, time to
    dose into the circular-arc
        of sleep

long enough to forget that you
     pleased me highly, that we resisted
               openly
as care brims as care dwindles, though it must
          mean something: never have let anyone else
               stroke my hair

O EXCLUSIVE WEAVE

the pigment of the early past,
more smoke than burn,
has been cleared away

like swept snow, overturned;
you sit thinking of the rest of them
in cinders of promiscuity

of Don Juan, in mid-evening
as merry as black cherry
as he sits on the wine-cask,

by noonday forgetting your name
like entry erased;
one dream to select and be

selected, o exclusive weave,
beyond the blithering bland
named unfinished, momentary

when will you be the only face
for me? when will I be
the only face for you? one

to one, where each
entirely renders
in turn, in return;

for the fruits
that the fewest have
are the most tasty

RETREAT

Retreat, apart from detail
  against a guise, glass houses and
the urban crust, retreat
  against difference and sameness
against useless advances
  so that our fingers are now
ten thimbled thumbs, retreat
  silent like the three-year-old
refusing to greet grandma, retreat
  against the taskmaster, the tatty crowd
against the hog or toga-judge
  retreat and repeat it, though
for good measure, as a rallying-point,
  we'll build an outhouse for the farm
and for the church
  new organs from old pipes, swiped

BREECH-LOADED VAMP

breech-loaded vamp
was content as an old clam
with her powder-puff enginery
she kept the old fellow going
till another man hit her tracks
who danced the mazurka
in triple time, brought her
meadow saffrons and bought up the town
but she still kept the old fellow going
till she knew she could fasten the man
as you'd couple railway vans
and only then did breech-loaded vamp
in charge of clack, throttle and vamoose
play the jilt
for only naturally, she had wanted somewhere
to land before she jumped

TUNNEL-BORERS

wives, we are the tunnel-borers
bearing light forward: after
darkness is the nasty fall
which love can make;

insolence is the catchy tune
which has pasha and wife
tug within the tumbling-box, hard
at home; each lies unrelenting,

still, deep inside the flue
of scrutiny, who will give in?
scrub clear the passage through
that solid hill? pride

has taken us numbly
by the scruff of the neck;
in due time, woman usually
twists her sentiment round

like a screw; in the meanwhile,
wives, even if we're angry
we should never pass an evening
without kissing pasha goodnight

CACHE OF HEAT

When like a singer on stage
who collects the bouquets and chairs
you hold firm the fly-fishing
microphone, he then is yours
at the grapy girdle junction—
      it has taken all
      your woman's cunning
      to get him this far
You tend by force towards him
      like a seasoned green linnet
      who's relieved him of his guesswork:
      Will she? Can I? Could we?
Till the cache of heat
is dry, till his grid is
a drop-scene under your
      spawn-hatching frame

FIGHTING WORDS

on a platform, on a stage flat
as grass sheared like sheep shorn

they play their parts to catch their
cause on the set: he, who prefers

life in books to life with bonds
and life with bonds to life in bars

toils for the disabled; she
goes all out to stop the rot

of native cultures, fighting words!
with the even rap of tap shoes

while out there the listeners turn
a deaf ear until he pulls

her skirt's fullness to the back,
only then do the purple-eyed oglers

clap their clefts or pudgy puds,
as she tends to draw herself to him;

for them,
there's no missing this scene!

HOUSEWIFE HOVELLER

Housewife hoveller! your day is carried
by twenty tapeworms: at breakfast 8 a.m.
you're blinded by the grapefruit-splash,
hubby is as cranky as an unfed tot,
dishes pile up like bird-droppings,
something's always too heavy or too hot,
only the five-minute-coffee allows you
to collapse into yourself

and then another violation of wholeness
like the sin of snot on the book page,
you ask yourself what on earth
you are to do about your overdrawn
bank account? you're as indecisive as
the girl who's kept up a fiancé
for six years till at last,
between the spaces, it's 8 p.m.

Grey as grandfather
the late lingerer, without account,
pats you on the shoulder
as he leaps fences through the front door

with women
fidelity like a ring;
with men
fidelity like a snowflake

NO DEATH BUT MOURNING

She had reached the point wherein the slightest
noise was unbearable but worse still, there seemed
nowhere to go; worse still, she could only regret
that she couldn't leap out of her skin, just for a
day, just for an hour, couldn't someone come and
help. Perhaps that was too much to ask. Not to
worry about longevity. Entitled to peace. Yes. O
that kind of dream. She couldn't even feel the morning. She would have prefered a million other lives.
Just to leave the skin a minute, please. Little
dishevelled lustre. No death but mourning. She was
going under, out-and-out, like a boat under bridge
too tight for its body. Her downfall was like that
of a great ruin which the government didn't think
worthy enough to preserve. She had split from herself.
Was encrusted in the blown circle with no hope to
be unshackled. Numbed loop, bolt, bow of padlock,
coupling link which fissures, hole of impediments. To
spend the last day like a beggar. Perhaps one single
hosanna would rise from the horizon. But she could
not leave her skin; it had been eaten.

MOTHER SUPERIOR

Steadily, Mother Superior
in rearing her chickens
formed the shell's inner

chicle; she put them
to nurse with rhymes
"Frog and hog and Mrs. Wren

put daisies round
their garden pen . . ."
on days when they had

sleepy, sickly, hissed at
heads; how she healed
with quilted hushabies.

once pony and pudding
dreams, clean loom and lock
of starlings' safety

when, abruptly, age filed in
the spank was done
and woman sat to woman

as equals, while the sides of love
held the balance and there was
no losing hold

till time took in its muzzled
sail further; Mother
Superior stooped and sunk, now

they put her to nurse
with rhymes for every child
becomes her mother's mother

POETIC JUSTICE

The only way that she can come to you
tonight is in the coffin; this is

a spacious shutting away. Why
was the child not touched enough?

Now she is permanently closed, barbed
like wire, even a pot-boiler

will not earn her a living;
how short the song of gondolier.

Undisguised, ill-provided, she is afraid;
perhaps at this moment, you are already

trapping other hands with
a creeping barrage of calculated shells.

Just remember that she held
a title in her own right. Gone

the haggling over terms of give and take.
The sun flattens them out

with its swizzle-stick rays;
the long-billed hummingbird swings

like a spinning top at the cliff's face
till its balance is knocked off blaze

while its low hum loses a clef.
The barge-pole shifts, has a slack rein

on the flooded tract of land,
teeth chatter; the children have left

their knick-knacks and toy boxes on the bank.
They are not able to keep their heads

above water, they swallow the sinking waste
paper, recklessly, but of course you know

all the poets have jumped into the sea

KELDAY'S LAST NIGHT

And Mary Kelday died at age fourteen, she whose love
had gone as far as lip's tip on father's fair forehead
or perhaps as far as a joust with the neighbour's boy;
one kiss seamed and shaped and I'll give you a zinnia,
he hollered. Kept as a sleeper to the sharp edge, to the
headstone's haphazard wedge, she is not yet dead. Her life
is re-entrant here, as I roll out the woodnotes from summer
camp: her hair shot in short wild drops as she skinny-dipped
off a stony patch, as she leapt with her horse, kite-
converted, over each new jump; she was Algonquin Park's
jumping-bean queen, Buchaneerish Mary. Dimple-dented,
fair as arbiter. She even filled the bodice of a peasant
blouse and at that was an early woman neatly tucked together.
No justice in this world. She's out of hand now, disbudded,
disbranched. The nails have closed her in, air-tight; she's
made a rapid dash. Wheels screech. Wheels scribe. Wheel-silence.
Regrettably, she is vegetable rock and yet her life is
re-entrant here. We are connected
by her rush of blood in my head, by her
yearning virgin's clump. Like-minded we rally,
clump-souled. Mary, I will be Woman for both of us.

THE ROUND GAME

You hold the bundle of laundry
like a bundle of baby
and you pretend, by wearing
pillowed frocks heaved up
that you have bulging out in you
a Neville or Natasha;
it's a kind of round game
that has become a part of you
because it is a proud day
for you to know that
one man holds the bulb
and broth of your sensations
in his protective custody,
so you feel it is about time
that you stick out with him
inside of you,
with the man's timely care
of arms rounding you,
while more and more
these forms are pronounced
with round vowels and are real;

What is that burning in your oven, now?

OUR SIB'S RIBS

their bellies reach their hag-like
knees, their legs are thin as pencils
so that small garters would drop
easily down, these are the hungry children
who take to eating green bones
of fish without a dish, if at all
while we shoot our calves
and bury them, lop off
feed from our sib's ribs
with a gastric gash, while we,
under our over-refined, leguminous roof,
try to decide how to grill and grub up
the pulpy flesh-pots,
decide how much candied peel to add
to the mincemeat served steaming hot

CHILD I KNEEL TO BE YOUR SIZE

Child
you own your own
little room, a candle's passion
high, taller than I,
where sausage-shaped goblins rise
up from the nightshade's red rim

Child
with eyes full and rolling
Look! See! Behold! you have
wings as long as petrels,
you hide your stories in your slippers;
I will grow up to be a child, as you

Child
if I lay your picture out
will you return to me?
snatch me back
again? or has all your milk
been sowed, supped, and soured?

Child
if I promise to be good
will you extend your curious palm
to comfort me, to tow me
from the bitter stream?
child I kneel to be your size

IN THE HOUSEMAID'S PANTRY

From the time he dribbled, son loved
mother and as it happened, mum loved
son even more; she taught him to tie
a shoe lace as if it were a closely
fitting corset, to gobble the goodnight
kiss as if it were a rush on gold;

she'd stay about when she should have
gone out, she was at him with a twist
of insistence. He grew to prefer a cupful
of teat to a motor-car toy, he grew
to need her perfumed hankies in order
to sleep, he grew to copy her stately

graces in the housemaid's pantry. She
would have pledged her life for her
child, would plot and plod for him.
He had become her; wads of coil wade through
the vortex of the heart to the roof of mouths
and nothing can tear them out.

FREEDOM LASSO

the lasso is the loin of every lad
noosed around the first waist
which comes along, like line and hook
loosed, and around the next without delay;
so passes the lasso like light
from grandpa to pa to son

the lasso is the freedom of every man
to shun the roping of crotches
as notches, to measure the meaning,
it will not have what it cannot hold
to twin the sap, to complete one thing
is masterful, enough

the lasso is the longing of every old-timer,
when time the maker becomes time
the taker; it was the bone
that grew a tree that greened
a summer's center
till its stout leaf was pulled down

may the lasso be your skill
at ropemanship, a bearer's need
may the fastener of fruit
be the keeper of lasting seed

WHO ARE THESE MEN?

Who are these men?
who drill into the public purse
as if it were royal land not only held
by but made by sweat of State

Who are these men?
whose wrong-doings are swept
under the patched red carpet until the
dust fills an entire room

Who are these men?
who wear dark glasses as they pull
into the A-1 hotel with an unmarked key,
as they pull into Dame Jane's knee

Who are these men?
who do their best to do us better
one day up the tide, the next out of fashion
along with their fast-paced rib of words

Who are these men?
who ask how much? how long?
how far? how come? and how to hide it?
you've guessed, haven't you?

why, the local politicians

THE LAST PUFF AT HER PURITY

as a seventeen-year-old man
I know exactly what it's like:

the ones who are willing
you don't like,

the ones who you like
are unwilling;

and it's not simply that you
wish to take the last puff

at her purity, in fact
you wish to be thickly set

in knowing her, in completeness;
after school, just to tread

on open ground and undeniably
to seek a kind of quartz-beauty, like

a young sardine is only good
once the tin's been pried free

GOD'S GIFT

You think you are
God's gift to government
God's gift to man
God's gift to woman
God's gift to history
God's gift to poetry
When God's gift is to extinguish,
Indistinguishably

O BOGART

cynical you
with sneering dispatches, a scholar's
escape
     you have become the judge
of sweetness
sweetheart is sweet-sop
     you won't give in an inch
to *eau de rose* sentimentality
     you wrap *Ma Griffe* gifts
in old newspapers
     you refuse to write letters,
a compliment comes like Christmas
once a year O Bogart and yet
I'm the only one
     you honour with a grain of respect;
other people are levelled by
     your comic eye, leafbud of uncropped
potato, but I who once thought
     you were a window that would not lift
have deciphered your chin's graffito
     from façade to face, have
upturned your earth with a crescent-bladed spade
     and in so doing
     you know that I am
no homeless and helpless waif
for I have cracked
     your cynical shell
like dynamite an untapped safe

YOUR SPIRIT AS A REAPING-HOOK

Like the army's chief who strides ahead
by himself, the inner man is very much

alone. In shapes of dreams its stored grain
is oat to brain firm as the horny casing

of a horse's foot. It makes land
into islands, turns clay into desires

not always within shooting-range; it
refloats you when sunk, a further trump;

it's a plant's true skin beneath the cuticle,
when all else fails the inner man

prevails; how wide to wing?
how far to see? before it wears the willow,

time's chaff and chain mail? Forward
uttering children, be yourself, by yourself

for if you swing into your innerworld
wedge, they say your spirit

as a reaping-hook will never run out

THE RAW SNAPPING OF THE YEARS

white gloves, black beret
and walking-stick, stumped
neck, sloping shoulders

and tilted head; this is the you
you never thought you would
become. all the weight falls

to your right leg when you walk
and if the wind with its long
girders blows off your hat

you hesitate to force your back
out of straightness and when at last
you tighten up and bend, resolutely,

you then recall the newly married
man you once were,
your stalwart frame and upright wits –

'tis the raw snapping of the years;
sometimes the mind refuses
what the body must admit, you moan

when out of a ditch, a child from whom
you'd expect better deeds, tosses at you
a fast-moving, weathered stone

OLD MAN OLD TETHERING

If you were half as much morning
As I night

I would have you be here
To adorn me with white festoons, to trim

You to the pasture's height of youth, pup up
A perpetual lease, so that you would

Never have to yield to the old man
In you, to the old tethering, that flat rule

When your knees, curving downwards,
Would otherwise be checked by the fetterlock

Of time; if you promise not to hang up
Your fiddle when you come home, I shall make

Far-reaching efforts, as the clocking hen,
To stop the clock, to save you from

A closing: the mild, lipless kiss
Of wooden-soled space under wet ground

EACH LUCKLESS WIGGLE AND THE WIDOW'S PEAK

Too many have thrown dust in the eyes
      of those who go it alone
      crying halves though too old for breeding;
      in their wild locks hang
      each luckless wiggle
and the widow's peak

Through the keyholes staring
                    sit the men
Who count the butts and buttocks
                    in their pen

The stools strap them in, they're pinned
      as if to their place of origin,
      with no key, wedge, or bolt to pin
      the ones they could have loved, even
      the hired girls who thought that
upon a spindle, gold could the men whorl

Through the keyholes staring
                    sit the men
Who count the butts and buttocks
                    in their pen

How is it that they'd failed, flagged
      like unused fag-ends,
      while their man-hours were turned
      as thin as chin tufts so that
      whatever they touched, which others
took and tuned, they lost invariably

Through the keyholes staring
                    sit the men
Who count the butts and buttocks
                    in their pen

Like to like, these chamber-fellows line
        the room with blighted revenues,
        with what they should have said
        as a tribute to the dead
        upon whom their attention is still
fastened, as a gulp of guilt to regret

Through the keyholes staring
                    sit the men
Who count the butts and buttocks
                    in their pen

Into the stoppered glass bottle, they pour
        false sentiment and fasten the plug
        as tight as might some shaggy gents;
        onto their whisky pots
        they clench, white-lipped and
weaned, they are true to themselves

Through the keyholes staring
                    sit the men
Who count the butts and buttocks
                    in their pen

How endless is that age, how early is the end
    how unending the need for heart-throb,
    death is love nipped in the bud
    for those who know
    that depth takes time
and time for them is sick and short of breath

STRANGERS NEED BROAD SMILES

You stall by a bookstall
Because you've seen a stranger who is

Pretending to read; now who is this?
A man to sprout and spread or one to shrivel

Up and scuttle off, as his eye half sweeps
The page, half sweeps you, hurrying

To see if you are all flush and freshness
Or mostly shrew-mouse; his long shadow

Bends over your short shadow like intersecting
Bedclothes. Strangers need broad smiles,

Need to show at a glance their
Under-skin, even if a shy spell reduces

Their mouths to stalemate; before the plot
Is lowered to cackling slapstick, you bring

A leg forward. He stares, you dare, he blinks,
You wink and you walk away, hand in hand

FOR SOME FOR OTHERS

for some people the sun
is yellow a house is square
grass is green and the river
wet, for some people day
follows night, the seasons
are four, a desert is dry
and silence must be broken
but for others
the sun is security, always
going forward, outward, unlike
love, it cannot fall through, a house
is a spherical ball where
upside down is always
the right side up, grass is where
they leave lip-prints like footpaths
in the best of summers, the river
a piece of melting vegetation is
their life-line as sure-footed
as death's likelihood, but for others
the day becomes the night, the night
becomes the day (away all sequence)
the seasons are as many
as are dreams, each desert is not
barren but bearing monarchs
out of tree-toads, and silence
(an hour's only ecstasy)
is avid to remain silent
and with meaning

LIKE RIFF-RAFF UNDER RAIN

To feel none of anything
Neither length of pain
nor haste of love

when every eye is closed
or turned away, when emotion
is tubed with thinness like

a spectre-bat is slender to its
fingers. When even the fat meat
of memory has the shrunken look

of cut string. No one gives
special attention: that bread
and wine to your on-going mind

has put in a cease fire. No one
to rush through your day for, to
watch through rose-coloured specs.

No one to have you kick up
a light heel, keenly. No one
to risk loss for, no one to tease

your nostrils to the height
of goodly rage. When even your scores
of dreams are outlines wanting finish.

When even the slightest commotion
will do; when even the ragged robin
of a woman, once the poor man's

solace, will do, if she can
drive in fullness
and stuffing, if she can

plug your holes,
be covering to your treeless
plot of ground as soul.

To feel none of anything
Neither length of pain
nor haste of love

when your spirit is picked
of notable stirring, till it falls
over like riff-raff under rain.

DRAGON TREES AND WAWA POTS

Under the leering light of Wawa's Great Goose
she stirred the street, a stranger, eyes

like chisel-spears turned and stared;
up and down the striplings would strut

but her stem made them miss their step, that day.
Girls would drag anchor at every corner, the air

was wet with their stong-smelling lure
they stopped by a sewage hole, in drabbets,

to dream of four-horsed private vehicles.
But there now the blond man drew up, with photos

of fat roots and dragon trees, he led
her down the red orbed bush trails.

Did you know that there are
twenty-five kinds of earthly orchids

in Northern Ontario? They found five, playing
detective with a camera and reference book.

The magpie on Spring run-off
took a life that year, they managed

to dump the canoe in the first set
of rapids, heads poppled in order to duck

the club of wood clapping
like a wind-rattle scaring birds.

At the Art and Craft Show, their hands
peeled kiln-dry,

they had pot-roasted so many pots,
out-stripping daylight with their clay genus

hating to relinquish even an hour
to sleep; sometimes, they made a mattress

of spinning-wheels and spun rope-yarns
into spinal accord. By summer's end

it was time to bring out the chain saw
and plane down slabs of cedar tree,

it was time to grain out a cradle
for the expectant pleasure pot.

NO. 46 GORDON SQUARE, BLOOMSBURY

no. 46 Gordon Square, Bloomsbury
is where we live aunt and shadow and i
my space is a box with a balustrade
when i'm at sea at sea in the coffee cup
every night i have three appointments
with the scalp of sky; am the eccentric
crinkled sphinx
who could possibly shield me
from myself? while my malignant half
makes love in the nearest church,
the better half turns the hour in the hansom
from presentiments to words; my real name?
why the cannonball has splintered
its very brick; when i fell from the balustrade a draught caught me and up up
into the night swung the rolling
carved head minus mast toward
that other body (o slight white double
canopy) minus mask till
we were one. gentlemen. who can
shield me from my rocketing or
shall i age an air-born unicorn?
(can't i scare you with my lion's tail
and goat's beard?)
the silent back of a chair? or even
the veil upon the mourning muscle

fumbling like the finger which has lost
its hand? i'd give my entrails
for an ounce of real confiding away
away nameless voices you undress
the woman in me somehow my face
has caught on thick fire 'tis energy enough
no. 46 Gordon Square, Bloomsbury or
who could understand such stuff?

BEAUTY INTO BEING

the mind transforms beauty into being
so that we no longer want
     our eyes to see without being seen
     nor our summer to spring away
so easily; can lavender
     be that sweet
     and the bay that still
                afterwards
as the mind transforms beauty
     into being
lip to love
     rapidly
   with or without words,
    it is not the whisper nor the worship
but the I want to give of me;
     can the rain be that beautiful
     and the petal's closing
        not the gesture of refuge,
     to perceive that it is hardly
       strange to be
             more
    than what one is unto oneself;
that the poet breathes dreams
but that the dreams breathe life
    is both timeless
        and dependent
      on our space

ACKNOWLEDGEMENTS

Grateful acknowledgement is made to the *Canadian Review*, the first literary magazine to accept my work for publication;
to Nancy Cole, who was responsible for my reading a selection of these poems at the Edinburgh Festival (1975).

CF